The Magnificent Tower

Especially for Matthew and Patrick
Stephanie Jeffs

For Alison, Emma and Katie
Steve Hicks

Edited by David Martin

BIBLE SOCIETY
Stonehill Green, Westlea, SWINDON SN5 7DG, England

Published in association with AD Publishing Services Ltd
7 Hill Side, Cheddington, Leighton Buzzard, LU7 0SP

First published 1991

ISBN 0 564 08145 0

Printed in Hong Kong

The Magnificent Tower

Story by Stephanie Jeffs
Illustrated by Steve Hicks

'And finally,' said the Page, unrolling the last section of his scroll, 'the Prince of the Southern Lowlands has just unveiled a statue of himself which can be seen for fifty miles!'

'Enough!' boomed the King. 'I don't want to hear any more!' He rose from his throne and snatched the scroll from the Page. 'Last month the Prince held a royal banquet, the month before that he had an open day to show off his Funsplash swimming pool... I don't want to hear any more about the Prince of the Southern Lowlands!'

'Well, Sire,' stammered the Chancellor, 'the Prince is a very rich man.'

'And the Prince,' shouted the King, 'is only a Prince and I am a King! I want to do something so magnificent, so tremendous, that people will talk about *me* for a change! I am sick and tired of hearing about the Prince of the Southern Lowlands!'

With that the King plucked the crown from his head and flung it high into the air. The court gasped.

'I have an idea!' said the King slowly. 'I've got a brilliant idea! I will build a tower so tall, so spectacular, so monstrously, hugely tall, that from the top of it I will not only be able to see all of my kingdom, but I will look right into the Land of the Southern Lowlands!'

'But Sire,' said the Chancellor, 'the cost of such an undertaking would be very,' he paused, 'costly.'

'I don't care!' said the King, stamping his royal foot. 'I don't care!'

'Sire,' said the Chancellor, 'the royal coffers are rather low at the moment.'

'Low?' questioned the King.

'Yes, low,' repeated the Chancellor. 'We have to pay several bills this month; the bill for the royal breakfasts, and the bill for the cutting of the royal toe nails... and then we are still waiting for the bill from the royal hairdressers for washing and grooming the royal ringlets...'

'Quiet!' snapped the King. 'I have made up my mind! I am going to start building this tower tomorrow!'

'I beg you, Sire,' pleaded the Chancellor, 'look at the royal coffers and see for yourself.'

But the King was not listening.

'Tomorrow,' he proclaimed in a loud voice for all the court to hear, 'tomorrow I will start to build the tallest, most magnificent tower the world has ever seen! And,' he said, glaring at the Chancellor, 'it will be finished within the month! Send for the royal messengers!'

That very day the royal messengers went to every village and town in the King's land. They rode through the country on fine, white horses and summoned the people to listen to the King's message by blowing on noisy and very expensive trumpets.

'His most Royal Majesty,' they declared in loud voices, 'has undertaken to build the tallest, most magnificent tower the world has ever seen!'

A special messenger was sent to the Prince of the Southern Lowlands. The Prince smiled when he heard the King's message. 'This is very good news!' he said. 'I would like to see this tower for myself! Send for the Keeper of the Princely Diary!'

'Send for the Keeper of the Princely Diary!' called the Page.

'Send for the Keeper of the Princely Diary!' echoed the Doorman.

'The Keeper of the Princely Diary!' shouted the servant standing in the princely corridor.

'Bert – the Prince wants you!' yelled the
sixth under-footman in the servants' quarters.
'Be quick about it!'

Bert jumped up from his chair, grabbed his jacket with the letters KPD stitched in gold thread on the sleeve and blew the dust off a large, red book, which was, of course, the Princely Diary.

He ran up stairs and along corridors until, at last, he reached the large oak door of the Princely Throne Room.

'Your Princeliness,' said Bert, slightly out of breath, bowing low towards the throne. 'Your Princely Diary!'

'Look and see if I have any pressing
engagements for a month's time,' ordered the
Prince.

'No, your Greatness,' said Bert. 'Your diary
is quite free.'

'Good,' said the Prince, turning to the
King's page. 'You may tell the King that I will
visit him in a month's time, and see this
magnificent tower for myself! I am sure it will
reflect the greatness and importance of your
King. Please tell him I said so!'

Back at the Palace the King had spent many hours in the royal attics trying to find his old building bricks. In the quietness of his royal bedroom he built tower after tower, chuckling to himself and saying in a grand voice, 'I am sure it will reflect the greatness and importance of your King. This tower will show what a splendid King I am. This tower will prove how wonderfully clever and brainy and marvellous and magnificent and...'

He was trying to think of another word for magnificent when there was a knock at the royal bedroom door.

'Who is it?' said the King, annoyed at being disturbed.

'Only me, Sire,' said the Chancellor, poking his head round the door. 'I'm sorry to interrupt you, but the Royal Bricklayer wants to see you!'

'Can't it wait?' growled the King.

'No, Sire,' mumbled the Chancellor. 'It's about the tower!'

The Royal Bricklayer bowed low before the King. 'Your Majesty,' he said, 'we have just finished laying the tower's foundations...'

'Excellent!' said the King, slapping the Bricklayer heartily on the back. 'You'd better get a move on with the rest of the building, the Grand Opening Ceremony takes place in a couple of weeks.'

'The problem is, Sire,' said the Bricklayer hesitantly, 'the problem is...'

'The problem is,' said the Chancellor firmly, 'the royal coffers are nearly empty.'

'Rubbish!' said the King.

'The fact of the matter is, Sire,' continued the Chancellor, 'you are skint!'

'Nonsense!' shouted the King, throwing one of his building bricks at the Chancellor. 'I'm a great and magnificent King! I can't possibly be broke!'

Some time later, the morning of the Grand Opening Ceremony arrived. The sun shone brightly. The King had declared the day a public holiday, so that as many people as possible could see his magnificent tower.

The tower itself had been completely surrounded by large screens, so that no one could see its full splendour before it was officially opened. It was rumoured that even the King himself had not seen the finished tower.

There was a loud fanfare. The people in the crowd stopped talking and strained to get a closer look. There was a clash of cymbals and the Prince of the Southern Lowlands walked slowly towards the front of the crowd. He paused, turned to the people and waved. They all cheered.

Then, accompanied by a great roll of drums, the King entered and stood alongside the Prince. The Prince bowed.

'Your Majesty,' he said in a loud voice for all the crowd to hear, 'I am honoured to be here today and see for myself your magnificent tower. I am sure it will show the world what a truly remarkable King you are!'

'Thank you!' purred the King, visibly swelling with pride. 'This has got him worried!' he whispered to the Chancellor, without moving his lips.

'It is my great pleasure,' proclaimed the King, 'to reveal for the first time the tallest, most magnificent tower in the whole world, which was built by the greatest King in the whole world. Me!'

There was another loud fanfare, a crash of drums followed by a clash of cymbals. Taking a pair of specially made royal scissors, the King cut the ribbon to lower the cover, and turned to face the crowd, ready to see the faces of his subjects, full of wonder and amazement.

The crowd gasped and then went silent. This was just what the King had expected. He bowed low ready to take their applause.

He still had his head bowed and was examining the stitching on his new royal shoes, when he thought he heard someone laugh. He shot upright and glared at the faces in the crowd. His eyes caught sight of an old lady, tears streaming down her face.

'Ah,' thought the King, 'my tower is so beautiful, people have been moved to tears! This is better than I had expected!'

Then out of the corner of his eye he saw a small boy stuffing a hanky into his mouth. He peeped round and saw people smiling. Finally he heard a loud snort and then everyone roared with laughter.

The King swung round to face his tower for the first time. He looked towards the sun, and blinked. Surely his eyes were deceiving him. He closed his eyes tight, opened them again and stared.

'What's happened?' he spluttered. 'Where's my magnificent tower?'

'This is it!' said the Bricklayer, stepping forward. 'You didn't have the money to make a good job of it!'

'But that's not a tower,' said the king. 'That's a wreck!'

The Prince of the Southern Lowlands stepped forward, raised his hand to silence the crowd and tried not to smile.

'Your Majesty,' he said, suppressing a giggle, and pointing to the bricks on the ground, 'what we see before us today reflects exactly the sort of King you really are!'

'Yes!' shouted a brave voice from the crowd, 'the sort of King who doesn't think!'

'Yes!' laughed another, 'the sort of King who can't add up!'

'In fact, your Majesty,' said the Prince smugly, 'the sort of King who should have spent much more time doing his royal homework!'

Credits

Story by Stephanie J⬤
Pictures by Steve Hi⬤

Based on something
much older...

27

The Story Behind the Story

'Let me tell you a story.' Teachers, parents and older friends often say this when asked to explain something. If it's a good story it will use things we know about to help us understand something more difficult or more important. Sometimes the story will include a riddle or puzzle to help us think more carefully. Many famous teachers have used this idea. Often the stories are called parables. The word means 'putting things side by side'.

The story you have read is based on a parable Jesus told nearly 2000 years ago. Many of the parables told by Jesus have become very famous. He used these stories to help people think differently about things.

He told this story to people who all too easily said they wanted to follow him and share in his work. Many of them, he was afraid, had not thought very carefully about it and would soon give up.

'If one of you is planning to build a tower, he sits down first and works out what it will cost, to see if he has enough money to finish the job. If he doesn't, he will not be able to finish the tower after laying the foundation; and all who see what happened will laugh at him. "This man

began to build but can't finish the job!" they will
say.'

Luke 14:28-30

Things to Notice
About the Two Stories

A lot of work was done on the tower but it did not achieve anything useful.

The size of the job was not appreciated by the one who started to build.

Despite his efforts the builder was only made to look small.

Thinking About It

'I want to do something so magnificent, so tremendous, that people will talk about *me* for a change!'

- *Why do you think the King wanted people to talk about him?*

- *What were his reasons for trying to build the tower?*

- *How can wanting to be the centre of attention change the way we behave?*

- *Is it wrong to seek attention?*

'I beg you, Sire,' pleaded the Chancellor, 'look at the royal coffers and see for yourself.' But the King was not listening.

- *The Chancellor tried to advise the King but the King would not listen. Why not?*

- *Why do you think the King refused to see for himself how much money he had?*

- *Is it easy to be blind to the truth?*

- *At what sort of times do we choose to ignore the truth? What happens when we do this?*

The crowd gasped and then went silent. This was just what the King had expected. He bowed low ready to take their applause.

❑ *The King saw only what he wanted to. He had made a very good job of deceiving himself! In what ways is it possible to deceive ourselves?*

❑ *How is it possible to see and hear things and understand them wrongly? What are the dangers of doing this – to ourselves and to others?*

'What we see before us today reflects exactly the sort of King you really are!'

❑ *What sort of King was he?*

❑ *What was his biggest mistake?*

❑ *What can we learn from this story?*